W9-AWZ-807

TRIANGLE HISTORIES

THE CIVIL WAR

THE BATTLE OF ANTIETAM

Chris Hughes

BLACKBIRCH PRESS, INC.

WOODBRIDGE, CONNECTICUT

Published by Blackbirch Press, Inc.
260 Amity Road
Woodbridge, CT 06525

Web site: http://www.blackbirch.com
e-mail: staff@blackbirch.com

Printed in China

10 9 8 7 6 5 4 3 2 1

Photo credits:
Cover, back cover, pages 6, 8, 16, 19, 20, 23, 24, 26: © North Wind Picture Archives; page 7: Corel Corporation; pages 9, 11, 18, 28, 29: The Library of Congress; pages 13, 25, 27: The National Archives; page 14: Blackbirch Press; page 17: National Portrait Gallery.

Library of Congress Cataloging-in-Publication Data
Hughes, Christopher (Christopher A.), 1968–
The Battle of Antietam / by Chris Hughes.
        p. cm. — (The Civil War)
Includes index.
        ISBN 1-56711-551-9 (hardcover : alk. paper)
1. Antietam, Battle of, Md., 1862—Juvenile literature. [1. Antietam, Battle of, Md., 1862. 2. United States—History—Civil War, 1861-1865—Campaigns.] I. Title. II. Civil War (Blackbirch Press).

E474.65 .H85 2001   2001001572
973.7'336—dc21

CONTENTS

PREFACE: THE CIVIL WAR

Nearly 150 years after the final shots were fired, the Civil War remains one of the key events in U. S. history. The enormous loss of life alone makes it tragically unique: More Americans died in Civil War battles than in all other American wars combined. More Americans fell at the Battle of Gettysburg than during any battle in American military history. And, in one day at the Battle of Antietam, more Americans were killed and wounded than in any other day in American history.

As tragic as the loss of life was, however, it is the principles over which the war was fought that make it uniquely American. Those beliefs—equality and freedom—are the foundation of American democracy, our basic rights. It was the bitter disagreement about the exact nature of those rights that drove our nation to its bloodiest war.

The disagreements grew in part from the differing economies of the North and South. The warm climate and wide-open areas of the Southern states were ideal for an economy based on agriculture. In the first half of the 19th century, the main cash crop was cotton, grown on large farms called plantations. Slaves, who were brought to the United States from Africa, were forced to do the backbreaking work of planting and harvesting cotton. They also provided the other labor necessary to keep plantations running. Slaves were bought and sold like property, and had been critical to the Southern economy since the first Africans came to America in 1619.

The suffering of African Americans under slavery is one of the great tragedies in American history. And the debate over whether the United States government had the right to forbid slavery—in both Southern states and in new territories—was a dispute that overshadowed the first 80 years of our history.

For many Northerners, the question of slavery was one of morality and not economics. Because the Northern economy was based on manufacturing rather than agriculture, there was little need for slave labor. The primary economic need of Northern states was a protective tax known as a tariff that would make imported goods more expensive than goods made in the North. Tariffs forced Southerners to buy Northern goods and made them economically dependent on the North, a fact that led to deep resentment among Southerners.

Economic control did not matter to the anti-slavery Northerners known as abolitionists. Their conflict with the South was over slavery. The idea that the federal government could outlaw slavery was perfectly reasonable. After all, abolitionists contended, our nation was founded on the idea that all people are created equal. How could slavery exist in such a country?

For the Southern states that joined the Confederacy, the freedom from unfair taxation and the right to make their own decisions about slavery was as important a principle as equality. For most Southerners, the right of states to decide what is best for its citizens was the most important principle guaranteed in the Constitution.

The conflict over these principles generated sparks throughout the decades leading up to the Civil War. The importance of keeping an equal number of slave and free states in the Union became critical to Southern lawmakers in Congress in those years. In 1820, when Maine and Missouri sought admission to the Union, the question was settled by the Missouri Compromise: Maine was admitted as a free state, Missouri as a slave state, thus maintaining a balance in Congress. The compromise stated that all future territories north of the southern boundary of Missouri would enter the Union as free states, those south of it would be slave states.

In 1854, however, the Kansas-Nebraska Act set the stage for the Civil War. That act repealed the Missouri Compromise and, by declaring that the question of slavery should be decided by residents of the territory, set off a rush of pro- and anti-slavery settlers to the new land. Violence between the two sides began almost immediately and soon "Bleeding Kansas" became a tragic chapter in our nation's story.

With Lincoln's election on an anti-slavery platform in 1860, the disagreement over the power of the federal government reached its breaking point. South Carolina became the first state to secede from the Union, followed by Mississippi, Florida, Alabama, Georgia, Louisiana, Virginia, Texas, North Carolina, Tennessee, and Arkansas. Those eleven states became the Confederate States of America. Confederate troops fired the first shots of the Civil War at Fort Sumter, South Carolina, on April 12, 1861. Those shots began a four-year war in which thousands of Americans—Northerners and Southerners—would give, in President Lincoln's words, "the last full measure of devotion."

INTRODUCTION: "THE SLAIN LAY IN ROWS"

★ ★ ★ ★ ★

Dawn broke damp and misty on September 17, 1862. In and around the small farm community of Sharpsburg, Maryland, Union and Confederate soldiers had been awake for hours, making final preparations for battle—checking weapons, writing letters, praying. More than 60,000 Union troops under General George McClellan had assembled in the woods and fields around Antietam Creek in Sharpsburg. Their mission: stop the northward movement of Confederate General Robert E. Lee's 30,000-man Army of Northern Virginia.

Union troops charge through the bloody cornfield.

As the sun burned through the mist, the morning silence was broken by the thunder of Union artillery firing at Confederate positions around the Dunker Church. Federal troops followed the artillery, marching toward Miller's cornfield, which lay between them and the high ground of the church. Suddenly the cornfield came alive as Confederates rose up between the stalks and began firing.

Union General Joseph Hooker ordered his troops to withdraw and turned his artillery on the cornfield. The exploding shells cut the cornfield like a giant blade, and at 9 A.M. the Union and Confederate forces met again. Less than 200 yards apart, soldiers in blue and gray "stood and shot each other, until the lines melted away like wax," in the words of a Union soldier.

Fighting raged over the field, with control changing hands more than a dozen times. Three hours later, 10,000 men lay dead and wounded in the field. The sun was not yet directly overhead, the battle of Antietam was not yet half over.

CONFEDERATES IN MARYLAND

★ ★ ★ ★ ★

The outbreak of the Civil War caught many people by surprise. Most people refused to believe that a full-scale war could occur between Americans. Northerners thought the South was bluffing and would soon rejoin the Union. Southerners, meanwhile, were confident that the North would eventually let them secede. Few people on either side believed the war would be anything more than a few minor skirmishes before both sides reached an agreement.

In July 1861, both sides brought their forces near a railroad junction called Manassas. This spot, marked by a river called Bull Run and only thirty miles from Washington, was the setting for the first major battle of the war. Confederates led by Generals P.G.T. Beauregard, Joseph Johnston, and Thomas Jackson (who would earn his nickname "Stonewall" during the battle), defeated a larger, better equipped Union force.

Fighting shifted away from the East briefly as Union leaders attempted to strangle the Confederacy by blockading their ports and attacking through the rivers in the West. Union General Ulysses S. Grant captured Fort Henry and Fort Donelson in Tennessee in early 1862. Then on April 6, 1862, Grant was attacked by Confederate

Fighting in the West was bloody in the spring of 1862 at the battle of Shiloh.

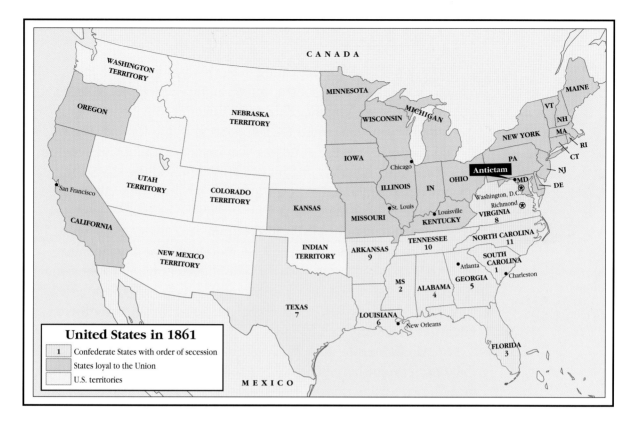

United States in 1861

1	Confederate States with order of secession
	States loyal to the Union
	U.S. territories

General Albert Johnston in the Battle of Shiloh. Though Grant managed to hold his position, the battle ended with almost 20,000 men killed, missing, and wounded on both sides. This enormous number of casualties was a clear sign that a long, brutal period of war lay ahead.

Back in the East, Union General George McClellan was making plans to attack Richmond, Virginia, the capital of the Confederacy. However, in a series of battles called the Seven Days Campaign in early summer, 1862, McClellan was surrounded and forced away from Richmond. Confederate General Joseph Johnston was wounded in the fighting and was replaced by General Robert E. Lee.

Lee had been one of the U.S. military's most respected leaders before the war. He had distinguished himself in the war with Mexico (1846-1848) and had led the troops who captured abolitionist John Brown in Harpers Ferry after his failed raid on the Federal armory in 1859. When the war began, President Lincoln intended to name Lee the commander of the Union army. When Virginia seceded, however, Lee felt that he had no choice but to side with his beloved home state.

Jefferson Davis, President of the Confederacy, hoped to make France and England allies.

★

Lee's Confederate forces captured Frederick, Maryland, on September 7, 1862.

★

Now, with McClellan retreating toward Washington, Lee moved his forces away from Richmond to attack Union General John Pope's army in western Virginia. Those two forces eventually met at Manassas Junction, and the result at Second Bull Run on August 29 and 30, 1862, was the same as a year earlier: a sound Union defeat.

This time, however, led by Lee and Stonewall Jackson, the Confederates planned to continue their advance into the North.

Lee realized that the Union's eastward retreat toward Washington had created an opening. He decided to move his army across the Potomac River into the Union state of Maryland. The Confederate leader hoped to accomplish three major objectives with this movement.

Knowing that Maryland was a slave state with many Confederate supporters, Lee believed the presence of his powerful army there might persuade Maryland to join the Confederacy.

Lee also wanted to move the fighting away from Virginia during the all-important harvest season to allow food and grain supplies to be gathered for his troops. The Shenandoah Valley was the "bread-basket" of the Confederacy, and much of the fighting for the first year had taken place there.

Finally, Lee wanted to convince foreign powers such as England and France to aid the Confederacy. Those nations relied on Southern cotton, and the Union blockade was hurting trade with them. General Lee and Confederate President Jefferson Davis believed that if they could show real success against the Union, England and France would pressure the North to stop fighting.

On September 4, 1862, Lee's Army of Northern Virginia crossed the Potomac and entered Union territory. Three days later, they captured the town of Frederick, Maryland. There, Lee decided to take a risk. He divided his army, sending two thirds of the men with Stonewall Jackson to attack the Union position at Harpers Ferry, Virginia. The Confederates could take the supplies and weapons from the Union stronghold, and protect their own retreat across the Potomac if they needed to. The other third of the army, under General James Longstreet, would move to the town of Boonsboro to hold off any attack from Union forces coming to reinforce Harpers Ferry.

Lee gambled by dividing his Rebel forces in Union territory. If the Union counterattacked quickly with a large force, the Confederates could be crushed. Still, Lee knew that General McClellan, commander of the Union forces, was famous for moving slowly and with great caution. Lee felt safe.

Then came one of the great mysteries of the Civil War. As Lee's soldiers left Frederick, Union troops entered the town behind them. In a field just outside the town, some soldiers found three cigars wrapped in a sheet of paper. Thinking the cigars were a great prize, the men almost didn't look at the paper. When they did examine it, they found something shocking. Written on the paper was Lee's order describing the division and placement of his troops. Called Special Order No. 191, the paper gave the Union army the chance to catch Lee unprepared and defeat him.

Jackson's Rebel troops destroyed a railroad bridge in Harpers Ferry early in the war.

Quickly, the paper was brought to General McClellan. As McClellan realized what he held, he told his aides, "Here is a paper with which, if I cannot whip Bobbie Lee, I will be willing to go home."

McClellan immediately brought his Union forces to western Maryland. He hoped to trap Jackson at Harpers Ferry and defeat Longstreet at South Mountain between Frederick and Hagerstown. Instead, his officers and his spies failed him. Thinking he faced a much larger force, McClellan was too cautious at South Mountain, and took an entire day to move past that point. At the same time, his men failed to trap Jackson at Harpers Ferry.

McClellan's movement surprised Lee, but news of Jackson's certain victory at Harpers Ferry convinced the Confederate commander to take a stand along the Antietam Creek near the town of Sharpsburg, Maryland. Jackson, meanwhile, after easily defeating Union troops at Harpers Ferry on September 15, marched his men seventeen miles to meet Lee. He left one division at

Special Order #191

No one has ever established exactly how an extra copy of Lee's orders for troop division was made. General D. H. Hill received a copy of Lee's orders, from General Stonewall Jackson, but never knew of a duplicate set of orders. Nor has it ever been explained why the order was left in a field, wrapped around the three cigars. In later years, Hill claimed that it might have been left intentionally by a traitor, but that has never been supported by any evidence.

When McClellan received the order, he began to move much more quickly than usual, but it does not appear that General Lee knew why. Some accounts claim that Lee knew of McClellan's find almost immediately, from a Confederate spy at McClellan's headquarters. Since Lee never mentioned it to any of his associates at the time, this is not likely. This error, which may have changed the course of Lee's invasion and perhaps the war, remains one of the great mysteries of the Civil War.

Harpers Ferry under General A. P. Hill to supervise the surrender of 12,500 Union troops and tons of supplies,

At Sharpsburg, Lee, Jackson, and Longstreet planned to make their stand. The Confederates had about 35,000 men lined up along a four-mile stretch between Antietam Creek and the Potomac River.

Throughout the days of September 15 and 16, they watched the Union troops assembling to fight. General Longstreet, recalling the arrival of the Union soldiers, wrote:

> The blue uniforms of the Federals appeared among the trees that crowned the heights on the eastern bank of the Antietam. The number increased, and larger and larger grew the field of blue until it seemed to stretch as far as the eye could see, and from the tops of the mountains down to the edges of the stream gathered the great army of McClellan.

Eventually, McClellan had over 75,000 men at Antietam. One of the fiercest battles in American history was about to take place.

America's Bloodiest Day

The area in which Lee had decided to stand and fight was a farming region of wooded, rolling hills. Its most visible landmark was a small white church of the German Baptist Brethren, called Dunkers. Antietam Creek wound through the east side of the battlefield. Because it was not very deep or very fast, the creek could be crossed by men and horses. Artillery, however, could not be pulled through the water. That made the three bridges across the Antietam very important—Union forces needed to use the bridges to move artillery into position and as a route for bringing reserve troops to the fighting.

The bridges over Antietam Creek were critical to the North for moving artillery into position.

McClellan planned a three-part attack. He wanted General "Fighting Joe" Hooker's First Corps to attack Lee's left flank from the north and General Burnside's Ninth Corps to cross the Rohrbach bridge and attack the Rebels from the south. With Lee's attention focused on his flanks, McClellan could send his cavalry across Middle Bridge and attack Confederates under Longstreet at the center with the remainder of his army.

13

Harpers Ferry

★ ★ ★ ★ ★

At the point where the Potomac River and the Shenandoah River come together lies the small town of Harpers Ferry. This town was in Virginia when the war broke out, though it became part of West Virginia when that state was formed in 1863. Because of its location, Harpers Ferry had been an important site for river and rail transportation. When a federal armory was built there in 1799, it became an important center for storing military equipment. The federal arsenal was the site of John Brown's famous raid in 1859 and became a frequent point of Civil War conflict.

Surrounded on all sides by cliffs, Harpers Ferry is almost impossible to defend. An attacking force occupying the high areas, can fire artillery down into the town without fear of a counterattack. Stonewall Jackson knew the area well, and when Lee instructed him to defeat the Union forces there, he did so with relative ease. He achieved the largest Union surrender of the entire war, taking 12,500 prisoners and tons of weapons and supplies.

The Morning Phase

At dawn on September 17, "Fighting Joe" Hooker ordered his Federal artillery to open fire on Confederate positions. The plan then called for Hooker's First Corps to cross Miller's cornfield and the areas called the East and West Woods. Confederate artillery quickly answered the Union guns from their commanding position on Nicodemus Hill. At 6:00 A.M. Hooker's men began an advance against the Confederates under Stonewall Jackson. General John Bell Hood kept his men in reserve in the Confederate center, ready to come to Jackson's aid if necessary.

The fighting was fierce. At one point, Union soldiers and Confederate troops stood 250 yards apart, pouring fire into each other. A Confederate private later wrote, "Never have I seen men fall as fast and thick…I never saw rain fall faster than the bullets did around us."

Miller's cornfield was one of the bloodiest spots of the battlefield. The Twelfth Massachusetts was one of many regiments that fought over that 20-acre piece of land. They entered the battle with 334 men, and lost 224. Their casualty rate of 67 percent was the highest of any Federal regiment that day. One young private described the fighting:

> It was rather strange music to hear the balls Scream within an inch of my head. I had a bullet strike me on the top of the head just as I was going to fire and a piece of Shell struck my foot - a ball hit my finger and another hit my thumb. I concluded they [were] meant [for] me… The firing increased tenfold, then it sounded like the rolls of thunder.

The Union's greater numbers eventually began to push the weakening Confederates back. Hood's men, who had just sat down to breakfast, dropped their food and raced into the battle. The impact of Hood's 2,300 fresh soldiers was "like a scythe running through our lines," as one Union officer described it.

Both Hooker on the Union side and Hood on the Confederate side lost thousands of men. Hooker called for reinforcements from General Joseph Mansfield's Twelfth Corps. On the Southern side, Hood lost 60 percent of his soldiers. Later, when asked where his men were, Hood sadly responded, "Dead on the field."

★

Fighting in Miller's cornfield in the morning killed thousands before the Union took control of Dunker Church.

★

15

The Dunker Church was an important position in the battle.

Though General Mansfield was killed in the fighting, Union forces crossed the Hagerstown Pike and took control of the Dunker Church. One Union soldier, fatally wounded, displayed his bravery when he said, "Well, I guess I'm hurt about as bad as I can be. I believe I'll go back and give 'em some more."

Both sides called for more reinforcements. General McClellan ordered most of the Union's Second Corps into the fight. General Edwin "Bull" Sumner prepared to lead his Federals into battle just as Robert E. Lee himself rode up on the other side to check the condition of Stonewall Jackson's forces. Realizing that the troops had been in heavy combat for several hours, Lee called up two divisions from General Longstreet to support Jackson's weary men.

On the Union side of the battle lines, Sumner's forces entered the battle with only a vague idea of how the Confederate lines were positioned. He relied on Hooker to give him accurate information, but when a Confederate sniper shot Hooker in the foot, "Fighting Joe" was lost for the day. Sumner sent General John Sedgewick's division straight across an area Sumner assumed was empty of Confederates.

Unfortunately, Sedgewick's men were lined up to fight an enemy in front of them when the Confederates were actually on their left. Turning to meet this attack, many Union soldiers found themselves firing into other Union troops in front of them. They suffered massive casualties from both friend and foe.

Antietam

Thomas "Stonewall" Jackson

★ ★ ★ ★ ★

Thomas J. "Stonewall" Jackson was probably the second most respected military leader in the Confederacy, after Robert E. Lee. He earned his nickname at the first Battle of Bull Run. As the Confederate troops prepared to retreat, one officer stopped his men by saying, "There is Jackson standing like a stone wall! Rally behind the Virginians!" The Confederates reversed their flight and won the battle.

Jackson became famous for his ability to march his men quickly through dangerous territory. At a time when most infantry covered 7 to 10 miles a day, his "foot cavalry" could march 25 miles a day or more, often without detection by Union forces. He became the hero of northern Virginia and the terror of the Union as he regularly swept through the Shenandoah Valley, sending the Yankees into retreat. After his capture of Harpers Ferry and fight at Antietam, Jackson fought at Fredericksburg and at Chancellorsville, where he was shot in error by his own men as he returned to the Confederate lines. Jackson's left arm was amputated that night. With little or no adequate medical care, Jackson died ten days later, at age 39, from his wounds.

"Angel of the Battlefield"

★ ★ ★ ★ ★

After traveling all night with a wagon full of bandages and other medical supplies, Clara Barton arrived at Miller's cornfield at around noon on September 17, 1862. Stunned by the enormous loss of life, she watched in horror as field doctors dressed soldiers' wounds with cornhusks. Army medical supply wagons had moved too slowly to keep up with the rapid movement of Union forces to the area around Sharpsburg.

Barton met some of the supply shortage by giving grateful surgeons a wagonload of cloth bandages and other medical supplies she had personally collected on her own over the previous year. Then, as bullets whizzed overhead and artillery boomed in the distance, Barton knelt by suffering soldiers, cradling the heads of some who took their last breath in her arms. She also prepared food in a nearby farmhouse for others and carried water to wounded men everywhere on the field.

As she knelt down to give one man a drink, she felt her sleeve flutter. Looking down she noticed a bullet hole in the loose cloth, then discovered that the bullet had killed the man she was helping.

Working without rest until dark, Miss Barton comforted the men and assisted surgeons with the grim work of amputation. As night fell, the doctors were stopped by lack of light. Barton pulled out lanterns from her wagon, and the men resumed their work.

For the rest of the war, the woman who later founded the Red Cross helped the sick and wounded.

"In my feeble estimation, General McClellan sinks into insignificance beside the angel of the battlefield," said Dr. James Dunn, a surgeon at Antietam, comparing Clara Barton to the Union Commander.

Sedgewick lost over 40 percent of his men and most of the land that the Union had gained. Sedgewick himself was shot three times before being carried from the field. His replacement, General Oliver Howard, later wrote, "the total loss of the division is 355 killed, 1,577 wounded (and) 321 missing...a record of almost unparalleled loss during a single battle. They have poured out their blood like water."

Sedgewick's troops came under fire from friend and foe.

The Bloody Lane

As the horrific fighting continued, Union General William French lost his position in the smoke and confusion. Seeing Confederate soldiers to his left, French decided to turn and move in to attack. Waiting were 2,500 Confederates under General D.H. Hill, who had dug into position along an old cart path worn by wagon wheels. These troops were the center of the Confederate army. If the Union could push them out, they could split Jackson's men from Longstreet's.

The cart path was a good defensive position, low enough for Confederates to remain out of sight until the Union soldiers came

★ ★ ★

"They have poured out their blood like water."
—Union General
Oliver Howard

★ ★ ★

19

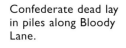

Confederate dead lay in piles along Bloody Lane.

★

In early afternoon, Union forces attacked the Confederate flank at Bloody Lane. By 1:00 they were at the center of the Rebel army.

★

over the top of the hill. This would make the Federals easy targets for Hill's men. This sunken road would become known as Bloody Lane.

Union General Max Weber led the first attack against the troops in the lane. As ordered, the Confederates held their fire until they could see the Union soldiers' belts over the top of the rise, then they opened fire almost point-blank. Weber's entire front line dropped, as he took 450 casualties in less than five minutes.

As French began to run of out of men to send, General Israel Richardson's men arrived. Led by a group known as the Irish Brigade, Richardson's men continued their attacks on the lane. The Irish Brigade took massive casualties, but rather than withdraw, they lay in the grass at the top of the hill and returned fire. When they ran out of ammunition, they took powder and bullets from the dead and wounded lying next to them, sometimes firing the dead men's weapons as well as their own.

The Confederates brought in reinforcements as their casualties mounted. Officers, often standing to rally their troops, were especially vulnerable. General George Anderson was fatally shot, and the next-in-command was killed minutes later. Colonel John Gordon of Alabama was shot in the face—his fifth wound of the day. He fell unconscious, face down in his cap. The only thing that saved him from suffocating in his own blood was another bullet that had torn a hole in his cap allowing the badly wounded officer to breathe.

Eventually, one of Richardson's Union brigades moved past the Irish Brigade and reached the Confederate right flank. It was like crossing a T. From that position, they could fire down the length of the lane, and pick off the Southerners. Confederates standing to meet the flanking fire were cut down by the Irish Brigade and other Union troops in front.

Antietam

One Union soldier described the events on this field: "The shouts of our men, and their sudden dash toward the sunken road, so startled the enemy that their fire visibly slackened, their line wavered, and squads of two and three began leaving the road and running into the corn."

As the bullets flew, one section of Alabama soldiers confused their orders and began to withdraw. Thinking they were being left behind, all the Confederate troops started pulling back. They left nearly 2,600 dead and wounded men in the lane. One Yankee wrote, "In this road there lay so many Rebels that they formed a line that one might have walked upon as far as I could see."

The Union "success" at Bloody Lane required three hours of brutal fighting and resulted in nearly 3,000 casualties. Now, however, the Union found themselves in a remarkable position. By 1:00 in the afternoon, they were in the center of the Confederate army, and could have pushed through to split Jackson from Longstreet. McClellan had plenty of soldiers at his disposal. Still, McClellan believed he was outnumbered by the Confederates and refused to commit more Union soldiers to the fight. As the fighting in the north and center of the battlefield came to an end, one of the greatest opportunities of the war was lost. Had McClellan attacked, the Confederate force might have been completely destroyed.

The Afternoon Phase

In the southern part of Antietam Creek, Union General Burnside had originally planned to launch an attack with his Ninth Corps at daybreak. His men, on the east side of the lower, or Rohrbach, bridge, made up the Union left flank. Their job was to cross the Antietam, strike Longstreet's men, and push through to Sharpsburg, cutting off any Confederate retreat toward the Potomac.

The area they were assigned, however, worked against their plan. Antietam Creek, four to five feet deep, was too deep for men to cross under fire. The stone bridge over the creek was 125 feet long and 12 feet wide. A steep hill on the west side offered Confederates a perfect view of any approach to the bridge, and the Union had no real cover on the east side.

"There lay so many Rebels that they formed a line that one might have walked upon"
— Union soldier describing dead Confederates at Bloody Lane

Ambrose Burnside

★ ★ ★ ★ ★

Although of similar rank, Union General Ambrose E. Burnside was very different from Stonewall Jackson. Before Antietam, he had been offered the command of the Army of the Potomac twice: once after McClellan's failure in the Peninsula campaign, and once after Pope's failure at Second Bull Run. Both times he refused because he thought he was not qualified.

At Antietam, Burnside was supposed to be in command of the First and Ninth Corps, which were stationed at opposite ends of the battlefield. Staying with the Ninth Corps, he was blamed for the delay it took to cross the Rohrbach Bridge. This delay allowed A. P. Hill to arrive in time and save the Confederates from being routed.

Despite that, when Lincoln replaced McClellan after Antietam, he pressured Burnside to take command of the Army. Burnside's command, however, lasted only through his terrible defeat at Fredericksburg. He then served under other generals with mixed success until his resignation in April of 1865. He served as governor and senator from Rhode Island after the war, and died in 1881. Ironically, one of the most lasting contributions Burnside made to history was in his facial hair. His odd side whiskers were called "sideburns" as a play on his name, and the term has stuck.

Burnside had sent a division to look for a better place to cross the creek, but the place they eventually found was two miles away. The 12,500 men of the Ninth Corps who were gathered at the bridge were opposed by only about 500 Confederates under General Robert Toombs. But Toombs had a much better position.

McClellan did not actually send the order to begin the attack in the south until almost 10 A.M. For the next two hours, Burnside sent several regiments at the bridge, but each was turned back with high casualties. Finally, Burnside turned to the Fifty-first New York and the Fifty-first Pennsylvania, both made up of tough and experienced fighters. The two regiments reached the path along the bridge, where they lay down and fired back at the Confederates. By now, the Georgia and South Carolina Rebels were running low on ammunition and began to withdraw. As the enemy fire let up, Union soldiers raced across the bridge. It was 1 P.M.—three hours after Burnside had been ordered to make his attack.

The first attack on the bridge over Antietam Creek lasted three hours.

Even though they had held off Burnside for hours, the Confederates now were in great danger. Burnside had over 8,500 soldiers available to him, in addition to the 10,000 Federals still with McClellan who had seen little or no action that day. Facing them were 2,800 Confederates under the direction of General David R. Jones. If the Union forces could break through the Confederate lines, they could reach Lee's headquarters at Sharpsburg. From there, they could cut off the South's path of retreat and trap them.

Again Burnside's planning failed him. His reserve regiments and ammunition were based almost a mile away. It took two hours to bring them all over the bridge and prepare for a final attack.

At 3 P.M., that attack began. Although the fighting was fierce and the Confederates held their positions as long as they could, the sheer numbers of Union soldiers slowly pushed them back. General Lee, watching the battle, ordered the ambulances full of wounded to move toward the Potomac, preparing for a full retreat. But then, a cloud of dust appeared on the southern horizon. His

★

By 3 P.M., Union troops had crossed Antietam Creek and were driving back Rebel forces.

★

23

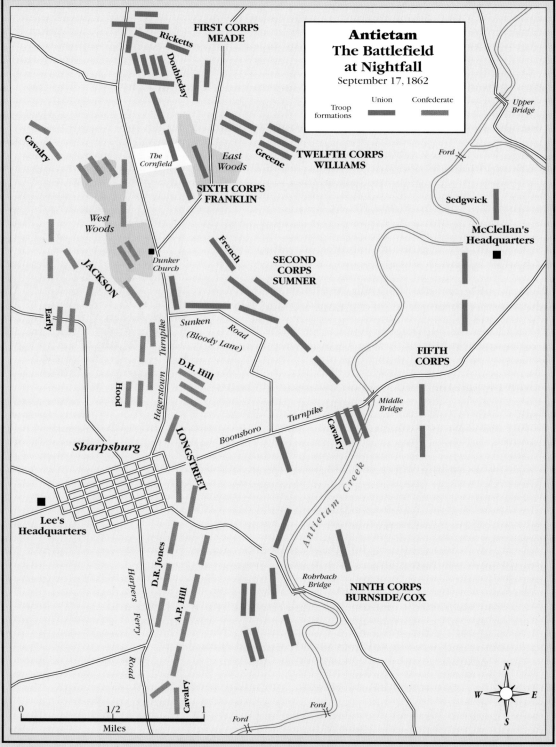

**Antietam
The Battlefield
at Nightfall**
September 17, 1862

Troop formations   Union   Confederate

FIRST CORPS
MEADE

Ricketts

Doubleday

Cavalry

The Cornfield

East Woods

Greene

TWELFTH CORPS
WILLIAMS

Upper Bridge

Ford

Sedgwick

McClellan's Headquarters

West Woods

SIXTH CORPS
FRANKLIN

JACKSON

Dunker Church

French

SECOND CORPS
SUMNER

Early

Turnpike

Sunken Road
(Bloody Lane)

FIFTH CORPS

D.H. Hill

Hood

Hagerstown

Middle Bridge

Cavalry

Antietam Creek

Sharpsburg

LONGSTREET

Boonsboro   Turnpike

Lee's Headquarters

D.R. Jones

A.P. Hill

Harper's Ferry Road

Rohrbach Bridge

NINTH CORPS
BURNSIDE/COX

Cavalry

Ford

Ford

0   1/2   1
Miles

N
W E
S

first thought was that a new Union division was entering the battle, and his army was doomed.

As the new soldiers approached, however, he recognized the flags of Confederate General A.P. Hill, part of Stonewall Jackson's corps. Hill had been left behind in Harpers Ferry to negotiate the surrender. Suspecting that his men might be needed, he marched them 17 miles to Antietam in only seven hours. Hill's men waded into the fight, surprising Burnside's Federals, and pushed them most of the way back to the Rohrbach Bridge. The Federals lost almost 2,000 men, compared to 1,000 lost by Hill and Jones.

As twilight fell, the crack of gunfire ended, replaced by cries and groans of wounded soldiers. The Battle of Antietam was over. The Union had gained a small amount of land—one mile on the Confederate left and half a mile on their right.

The price of those small gains was staggering. The Union lost 25 percent of the men who fought: 12,401 men killed, wounded, or missing. They also lost 20 officers, including nine generals. The Confederates lost 31 percent: 10,318 men, including nine generals and 22 other officers. The total of 22,719 casualties makes September 17, 1862 the bloodiest single day in the history of the United States.

The next day, September 18, could have brought an early end to the Civil War. Despite the heavy casualties, McClellan had thousands

Rebel troops were pushed back—until Hill arrived with reinforcements.

★

By evening, the Union had gained about a mile of ground.

★

George McClellan

★ ★ ★ ★ ★

After the failure of the Union army at First Bull Run, George McClellan was named commander of the Army of the Potomac in August of 1861. A graduate of West Point, McClellan was well known for his ability to organize and develop an army, and equally well known for his refusal to use that army aggressively. He failed to capture Richmond, driven back in the Seven Days Battles. Part of that loss, however, was due to typhoid and other diseases that struck the Union troops. He then lost command of most of his men when Lincoln shifted them to General Pope's army. After Pope's defeat at

Second Bull Run, McClellan was again given command. Though McClellan was respected by his men, many of "Little Mac's" troops began to lose their faith in him after the terrible losses at Antietam.

After that battle, McClellan was removed from command for his failure to follow Lee's army into Virginia and engage the enemy. When he did not receive new orders for a command, McClellan turned to politics. In 1864, as the Democratic candidate for President, running against Abraham Lincoln, he was soundly defeated. He served as governor of New Jersey after the war, and died in 1885.

of men at his command who had not yet fought, and he had many more within easy reach of Sharpsburg. Lee, meanwhile, had used almost all of his troops in the fighting. McClellan could have put more than 62,000 troops into action, half of whom were completely fresh. Lee, who had gained about 5,000 stragglers overnight in addition to A.P. Hill's men, had fewer than 33,000 Confederates, all of whom were exhausted and battered.

Both sides prepared for the final Union attack. Union generals made plans for their assault, and suggested plans to McClellan. The Confederates manned their posts, buried their dead, treated their wounded, and waited for the attack that never came.

McClellan, fearing what would happen if his men should lose, never gave the order. As night fell, General Lee took his men back across the Potomac and into Southern territory again. McClellan sent a small force after him, but they were stopped and turned back at Shepherdstown. The invasion of Maryland had ended.

The Aftermath

In military terms, the battle of Antietam was considered a draw. The Union lost more total soldiers, but the Confederates lost a higher percentage of their men. The Union made some small gains in territory, but the Confederates left the field by their own decision and in good order. Both sides lost much along the Antietam Creek, and both commanding generals took blame. Many in the Confederate

President Lincoln inspected Union officers and troops shortly after the bloody battle at Antietam.

★

On September 18, both sides prepared to continue the battle. Union General McClellan, however, never gave the order.

★

27

The Emancipation Proclamation

★ ★ ★ ★ ★

Abraham Lincoln had not planned to end all slavery when he first took office. By the second year of the war, however, he realized that he had to make a strong stand on the issue. When he drew up his first draft of the Emancipation Proclamation, many members of his cabinet were opposed to it. Lincoln wanted to use it, but decided to wait until he had some positive news from the war. He did not want the statement to seem like a desperate move. Although Antietam was not a Union victory, the fact that Lee was forced from Maryland was positive enough for Lincoln. He issued the statement, which freed all slaves in those areas still under rebellion as of January 1, 1863.

The Proclamation stated: "All persons held as slaves within any state or designated part of a state the people whereof shall then be in rebellion against the United States shall be then, henceforth, and forever free; and the executive government of the United States, including the military and naval authority thereof, will recognize and maintain the freedom of such persons."

Lincoln hoped that this might convince those border states either in the Confederacy or wavering, to stay loyal to the Union, since slavery was not being outlawed in those states. He also sent a clear message to England and France, who had been threatening to become involved on the South's side. Now, if they joined the conflict, they would be fighting to protect slavery, which was illegal in both those nations.

ranks came to regret Lee's decision to invade Maryland. One officer wrote to his wife, "Our Army has shown itself incapable of invasion and we had best stick to the defensive." Still, many Southern newspapers reported the battle as a Confederate victory, and Lee remained the unquestioned and beloved leader of his army.

More Americans were killed in one day at the Battle of Antietam than in any other battle in American history.

McClellan did not fare so well. He had been given a remarkable number of opportunities to defeat Lee, and he had wasted them all. Although he was one of the best-loved officers in the Union army going into the battle, even his strongest supporters realized that he had failed in his task. One Union soldier wrote to his family,

> *Why in the name of heaven McClellan did not let our corps finish up the 'rebs,' and why he did not renew the battle on Thursday, and follow speedily across the river, I can't understand . . . I cannot help feeling that this prolongs this horrid war.*

President Lincoln was among the general's critics, and he pressed McClellan to chase Lee and finish the job. When McClellan failed to move, Lincoln himself came to Antietam for a surprise inspection of the troops. McClellan still refused to move, and eventually President Lincoln removed him from command and replaced him with General Ambrose Burnside.

Beyond the military results, the Battle of Antietam favored the Union for several reasons. Lee's Northern invasion was stopped, and Maryland remained part of the Union. In Europe, England and France became concerned that the Confederacy might not be strong enough to win the war. The countries decided to withhold their support until things looked better for the South. That sign never came.

Perhaps most importantly, President Lincoln had been waiting for a positive event to issue a new policy. Although Antietam was not a clear victory, the withdrawal of Lee's army convinced Lincoln to act.

On September 22, the President issued the Emancipation Proclamation, which freed the slaves of the states still under rebellion as of January 1, 1863. With this act, Lincoln hoped to weaken the South by making them fear the threat of slave revolts. He also hoped to push the border states to rejoin or stay with the Union. Finally, he wanted to change the focus of the war from states' rights to slavery. That way, any outside force such as England or France would be less willing to help the South, since they would clearly be fighting to defend slavery.

The Civil War went on for almost three more years, involving millions of soldiers and killing more than half a million men. The Confederacy would be successful in battles for several months after Antietam, but at a high price. They lost men and supplies faster than they could replace them. Among the most serious losses was General Stonewall Jackson, who died after the battle of Chancellorsville in 1863.

The South reached its "high water mark" at Gettysburg, Pennsylvania, in a second invasion of the North in July 1863. Defeated after three days at Gettysburg, the Confederates also lost territory in the West to Union General Ulysses S. Grant. When Grant was brought east to take command of all Union armies, he began a slow, devastating push into the South which eventually brought about the surrender of Robert E. Lee at Appomattox Court House in April of 1865. The remaining Confederate forces surrendered soon after.

Although the battle of Antietam was considered a draw, it was one of the most important clashes in the entire war. It holds a key place in U.S. history. The modern weapons of war—rifled guns, conical bullets, and explosive shells—created unimaginable bloodshed. Never before or since would so many Americans fall in battle in a single day.

Yet Antietam stopped the momentum of the Confederacy, and gave Union soldiers confidence in their ability to stand up against battle-hardened Confederate troops. The outcome of the battle forced foreign governments to re-evaluate their position on the two sides, and it gave Union supporters much-needed confidence in President Lincoln's ability as a war president. Perhaps most importantly, Antietam allowed Lincoln to issue the Emancipation Proclamation, which helped change the perception of the war—at that time and throughout history.

Glossary

artillery large weapons used by fighting forces that fall into three categories—guns or cannons, howitzers, and mortars

brigade a military unit smaller than a division, usually consisting of three to five regiments of 500 to 1,000 soldiers

commander a military leader, usually holding the rank of general

corps a military grouping of between 10,000 and 20,000 soldiers

division a military grouping of between 6,000 and 8,000 soldiers or two to three brigades

feint in military usage, an attack on one part of an enemy's line in order to distract attention from the main point of attack

ford a crossing on a stream or river.

quartermaster officer in charge of providing food, clothing, shelter, and other basic supplies

regiment a military unit smaller than a brigade and a division. In the Civil War soldiers fought in the same regiment throughout the war with fellow soldiers who usually came from the same state, city, or town

reinforce in military terms, to strengthen a military unit by sending in fresh troops.

For More Information

Books

Clinton, Catherine. *Scholastic Encyclopedia of the Civil War.* New York: Scholastic, 1999.

Dolan, Edward. *American Civil War: A House Divided.* Brookfield, CT: Millbrook Press, 1997.

Hughes, Chris. *Antietam* (Battlefields Across America). Brookfield, CT: Twenty-First Century Books, 1998.

Stanchak, John. *Eyewitness: Civil War* (Eyewitness Books). New York: DK Publishing, 2000.

Web Sites

Antietam
> Learn more about the battle of Antietam and famous Civil War generals—
> **www.militaryhistoryonline.com/antietam/default.htm**

Antietam National Battlefield
> See photos of and learn more about the Antietam battlefield—
> **www.nps.gov/anti/**

Index